An Overseas Adventure:
Our Journey to Italy

by Clarissa Rachel

This Book Belongs To

_____

It was a bright, sunny afternoon when Mikaela's dad returned from work with big news. While Mikaela played with her cat Nino in the living room, her parents chatted in the kitchen. "Mikaela, come over here! We have some exciting news!" her mother called out.

Mikaela hurried over, and Nino followed close behind. "What's going on, Mom?"

Her father grinned. "We're moving to Italy!" Surprised, Mikaela's eyes widened. "Italy? We're moving again already?"

Mikaela felt comforted as her mother embraced her warmly. "I know this move might seem daunting, sweetheart. Just imagine the adventures that await you! You'll meet friends and explore new places," Mom expressed a hint of joy in her voice.

Glancing down, Mikaela noticed Nino nestled in her lap, purring with delight. With a smile, she gently stroked behind his ears. "Okay, Mom and Dad. Let's start our journey to Italy!"

The weeks that followed were busy with packing and goodbyes. Mikaela's room was filled with boxes. Nino had a time hopping in and out of them.

"I found you, Nino!" Mikaela said with a laugh as Nino popped his head out of a box. Saying goodbye to her friends was emotional. She hugged her best friend, Olivia, before saying goodbye. "I'll really miss you, Olivia."

Olivia put on a smile. "We'll stay in touch with tons of letters and video calls. Don't forget to tell me all about your adventures in Italy!"

Mom noticed Mikaela looked sad and gave her a comforting smile and a warm hug. This would be their second move since Dad joined the Air Force. The first move was from one base in the States to another. This time, the Browns were heading overseas!

Best Friends FOREVER

"Are you all set to head to the airport, Mikaela?" her dad asked. "I believe so. I'm feeling a bit anxious since I've never flown before."

The airport was busy and noisy. Mikaela held onto her father's hand firmly. She noticed the look of worry on his face. Concerned, she asked, "Daddy, are you okay?"

Her father smiled, though Mikaela could sense a touch of unease. "I'm alright, sweetie. Just not particularly fond of flying, that's all."

Mikaela was shocked. "But you've flown so many times!"

"That's true," he laughed. "But sometimes, even grown-ups get nervous."

Mikaela held her dad tight as they entered security and found their gate. "Don't worry, Dad. Everything will be fine," she said, hugging him tightly.

Mikaela squeezed her parent's hands firmly as they got on the plane. Seated by the window, she felt excited as the aircraft prepared for takeoff. As the plane launched into the sky, Mikaela gazed out of the window and watched the ground vanishing beneath—a blend of nervousness and anticipation filling her heart.

After spending hours in the air, Mikaela perked up at the sound of the pilot's announcement over the intercom. "Ladies and gentlemen, we are about to start our descent into Italy. Please make sure your seat belts are securely fastened." She leaned closer to the window, eagerly taking in her view of Italy. The sight was breathtaking! Lush green fields, winding roads, and brightly painted houses came into view.

When the family reached Italy, Mikaela was amazed by the town's buildings and charming narrow streets. Looking at her with a smile, her mother remarked, "Here we are. Our new home." Their lovely new house featured a terracotta roof and a cozy garden that brought comfort to Mikaela as she started to feel at home.

"Welcome to your castle, Prince Nino!" Mikaela exclaimed with a bow as he eagerly started to discover his surroundings.

Her parents assisted her in unpacking and arranging her room to her liking. That evening, as Mikaela lay in bed with Nino snuggled up next to her, she fell asleep dreaming of the thrilling adventures that awaited them in this wondrous place.

Mikaela and her family found the initial days in Italy to be quite busy. The Air Force base was full of activity, with numerous military families coming and going. The Browns were eager to get settled in their new home as quickly as possible.

The next day would be Mikaela's first day at school on base. She felt a mix of shyness and nerves. She was soon put at ease by her teacher, Mrs. Thompson's welcome. Before long, she made friends with Jake and Emma. At lunchtime, Mikaela sat with her classmates. She listened as they shared stories of their past bases. "I've lived in Japan and Germany," Emma proudly declared.

LUNCH TIME LUNCH LUNCH TIME

In the afternoon, the kids enjoyed a game of kickball during recess. Mikaela was excited to bond with friends who understood what moving from place to place was like.

Despite making friends, Mikaela faced some struggles with her schoolwork. She found the assignments to be tough and, unlike what she was used to at her old school, which left her feeling overwhelmed. One evening, as she sat at the kitchen table working on her homework, she let out a sigh of frustration and rested her head on the table. Her mom sat beside her, offering words of encouragement. "I know it's not easy, Mikaela. Just remember, you can always ask for help. Let's tackle this together."

With her mom's help, Mikaela slowly began to understand her assignments better. It was still challenging, but she felt more confident each day. Sometimes, Mikaela missed her friends and her life in the States. One day, after school, she told her mother, "Mommy, I miss my friends. It feels strange not having them," she said. Mom embraced her tenderly, saying, "It's normal to feel like this. Things will get easier as time goes by."

The family strolled through their town on weekends, enjoying the cobblestone streets and quaint shops. During one weekend outing, they tried gelato or Italian ice cream for the first time. Mikaela chose strawberry and declared it the most delicious ice cream she had ever had. "This is amazing!" she exclaimed with a sparkle of joy in her eyes.

Nino also had his share of adventures, including when he got stuck in the neighbor's olive tree. The whole family came together to rescue him. There was a lot of laughter and celebration once they managed to get him down.

The months seemed to pass by quickly. Mikaela had grown to love her new life in Italy. One evening, her father arrived home with some news.

"Hey, Mikaela," he greeted warmly. "We're planning a weekend trip to explore the Amalfi Coast!"

"The Amalfi Coast?" Mikaela asked with curiosity. "It's a beautiful place by the ocean," said Mom, "with plenty of sights and activities to enjoy."

Mikaela's eyes lit up with excitement. "That sounds amazing! I can't wait!"

The day of the trip arrived, and Mikaela woke up early, too excited to sleep. They packed their bags and set off on the adventure, driving through scenic countryside and delightful towns. Mikaela loved watching the change in scenery as they neared the coastline.

The ocean sparkled in the sunlight. The vibrant houses resembled something from a storybook. The family settled into a quaint hotel, and Mikaela was eager to begin her adventures.

Their first stop was a boat tour along the coast. The boat tour guide pointed out interesting landmarks and told fascinating stories about the area's history.

"Look at those cliffs!" Mikaela exclaimed, leaning over the side of the boat.

Her dad smiled. "And just wait until you see the caves. There's one called the Blue Grotto, famous for its glowing blue water."

As they arrived at the Blue Grotto, the water shimmered with a mesmerizing hue inside the cave; Mikaela felt like she had stepped into a fairytale. "This is absolutely magical," she murmured softly. That night, they joined in on a celebration in a neighboring village. The air was alive, with music, joyful dancing, and laughter. After the festival, Mikaela and her parents enjoyed a fireworks show above the sea.

One afternoon, after school, Mikaela found herself in her room, surrounded by her sketchbooks, colorful pencils, and sketches showcasing her latest adventures. Nino playfully batted at his favorite toy by her side. A gentle smile graced Mikaela's mom as she peeked into the room.

"How's my little artist doing?" she asked, taking a seat next to Mikaela. "I'm doing well, Mom," she replied, holding up a picture she had just finished. "Look, I drew the Blue Grotto from our trip!" Her mom admired the drawing. "It's lovely, Mikaela. You've captured it perfectly." Mikaela smiled proudly. "Thanks! I love it so much." Her dad walked in, carrying a scrapbook. "I thought you might like to add some of your drawings and photos to this," he said, handing it to her. "It's a way to keep all your new memories safe."

Mikaela's face lit up with joy when she received the scrapbook. "Dad, this is amazing! Thank you very much!" As she carefully placed her drawings and photos in the scrapbook, Mikaela thought about all the adventures she had since arriving in Italy. She remembered how nervous she was at first, but now she felt like she belonged. She had made wonderful friends and discovered the beauty of a new culture.

www.ingramcontent.com/pod-product-compliance
Lightning Source LLC
Chambersburg PA
CBHW041800040426
42447CB00001B/38